Published 1979 by Warwick Press, 730 Fifth Avenue,
New York, New York 10019
First published in Great Britain by
Angus and Robertson, 1978
Copyright © 1978 by Grisewood & Dempsey Ltd.
Printed in Italy by New Interlitho, Milan
6 5 4 3 2 1   All rights reserved
Library of Congress Catalog Card No. 78–68534
ISBN 0–531–09151–1 lib. bdg.
ISBN 0–531–09140–6

The Beaver

Story by
ANGELA SHEEHAN

Pictures by
GRAHAM ALLEN

WARWICK PRESS

The beaver was now two years old. She was one of the eldest of a family of beavers who lived together in a lodge made of mud and sticks. There were ten of them in all: father and mother, four three-week old kits, three one-year olds, and the eldest female. Her brothers of the same age had already left to live on their own. Now it was her turn to go. None of the others noticed as she swam to the bank.

The beaver sniffed the pine-scented air and cut a small branch from a felled tree. As she chewed its soft bark, she looked back across the pond. On the other side, her father and the older kits were hard at work. One was gnawing at the trunk of a tree, one was trimming a felled tree, one was hauling logs to the water. Her father was using the logs to enlarge the dam that he and his mate had started ten years before. The beaver turned and walked away into the forest.

The forest was darker than the river bank and strange noises came from the rustling trees. Owls hooted and coyotes howled. The frightened beaver could see almost nothing to start with. Then she saw a light glinting ahead of her. It was the fierce golden eyes of a lynx glowing in the darkness. The beaver froze. She was too far from the water to dive for safety. She could only wait for the cat to pass by. It came closer, but it could neither smell her nor see her dark shape. It yawned, licked itself, then padded away, silently.

Night after night, the young beaver wandered along by the stream. She slept by day in any safe hollow she could find. But in time she grew weary of walking and found a place where she could stay. It was perfect: a grove of trees, by a bend in the river. That same night, she laid claim to the river bank. She put her scent on heaps of mud and stones, and anywhere else that an animal would sniff. Any other beavers would know now that it was her home.

The very next night, she started to mark all the scent posts again. After a while she noticed a new scent. It was a good smell, but she could neither hear nor see anything to go with it. Then suddenly she saw a movement and heard a splash. She waddled down to the water and looked about. There, surfacing in the dim light, was a young male beaver.

He clambered out of the water and came towards her. She took in his warm smell and nuzzled up to his fur. She had been on her own for too long. It was time for her to have a mate.

When morning came, the beaver took her new mate to a hollow beneath a tree. There was just room enough for two. They snuggled up together and went to sleep.

Soon the days grew shorter. Before the leaves fell, the beavers would have to build a proper home. They had known how to cut and carry logs since they were born. One evening they set about damming the stream. Balancing on her tail, the female cut a notch in a tree with her sharp front teeth. Then she chiseled and gnawed all around the trunk.

At last she heard the fibers of the tree crack. She made a dash for the water as the tall tree crashed to the ground. Her mate, who was working on a nearby birch, only just managed to get out of the way.

The female then cut the larger branches from the fallen tree. Once the branches were off, she cut the timber into shorter lengths. Then she tugged and pulled the pieces down to the water. Her mate did the same with his branches.

The beavers started dam building by pushing the larger branches firmly into the bed of the stream. Next they wove smaller logs, branches and twigs across. They stuffed the gaps with mud and stones, which they clasped in armfuls to their chests. They piled up more twigs and brush for strength, and plastered them with more and more mud to make the dam watertight.

Slowly the water level began to rise. The beavers had dammed the stream and made a pool. Now they could make a lodge.

The beavers started the lodge by making a mound of mud and branches in the middle of the pond. After many days, it stood more than three feet out of the water.

Then they began to tunnel into the mound under the water. When their two tunnels reached the part of the mound above the water level, they hollowed out a big hole. They lined the floor with mud and made a bed of wood chips. Then they plastered mud over the roof, but left a gap with no plaster between the branches. This would allow in air for them to breathe. There was only one more thing to be done.

There had been plenty of food in the forest and the animals had grown fat. Their fat would help to keep them warm in the winter. But they would need fresh food as well. The mice, squirrels and chipmunks collected stores of nuts and berries. The beavers collected wood. When the pond was frozen, they would not be able to reach the forest. So they gathered a pile of branches and stuck them in the bed of the pond near the lodge. Now all was ready.

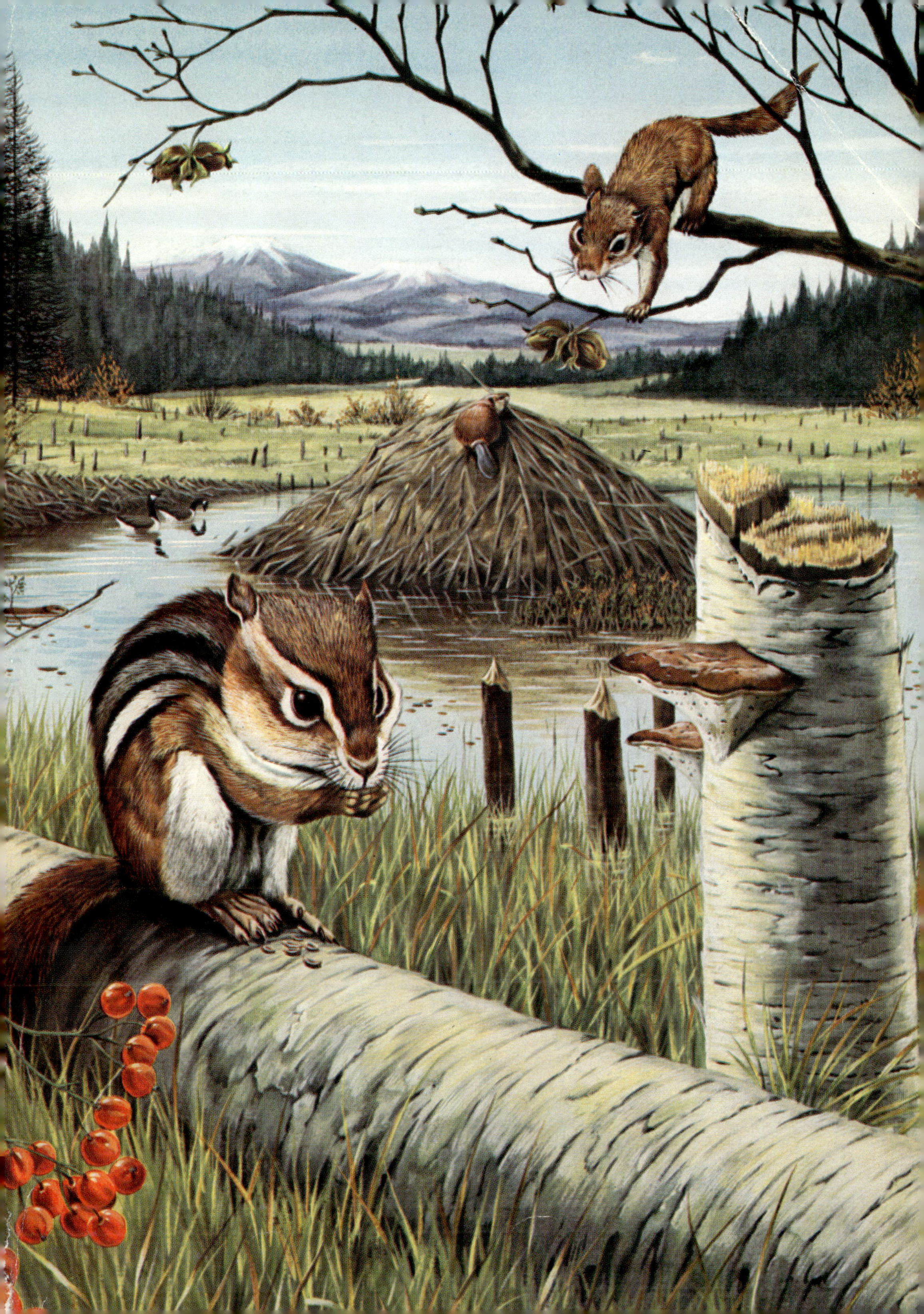

The last of the duck and geese flew south. Before long the forest was clothed in white. Under the snow, the ice on the pond was frozen so thick that the beavers could not crack it.

One sunny morning the beavers woke to a snuffling noise and the sound of claws scraping their roof. Through the branches in the airhole, they could see a patch of rough, black hair. It belonged to a bear, who was scratching at the walls of their home.

The beavers made ready to swim to safety. But they had no need. The walls were frozen solid. The great hairy beast could not break in. Throughout the winter other animals also tried to invade the lodge, but it was too strong for them.

At last the spring came. The ice on the pond cracked and melted. The beavers made their first trip to the bank. The green buds and leaves tasted delicious after the stale bark in their food store.

Chickadees and cardinals sang in the trees and frogs called to their mates. The beavers had mated already. It would not be long before the female had her first litter.

In the early summer, five tiny, fluffy kits were born. Their mother stayed in the lodge with them. They grunted and purred as she gently combed their fur and fed them with her milk.

After only four days, she led the young kits down the tunnel into the pond for their first swimming lesson. Their mother taught them how to rip leaves and bark from the twigs she brought them.

Each day the kits came out for a while with their mother. They floated and splashed in the water, and wrestled with each other. As they grew bigger, they started to cut and trim the young saplings in the grove.

One night two of them wandered to a distant clump of young aspens and started to gnaw at them. Suddenly came the howl of a coyote. The father beaver slapped his tail hard on the water. The two kits heard the warning, but only one was quick enough to get away.

The other stood facing the coyote. The terrified kit bared his teeth as the great animal sprang. The coyote missed him, danced sideways, and howled. Then there was another noise. The little beaver opened his eyes, and saw the coyote disappearing. A hare had bounded into its path, and it could not resist the chase. The beaver was safe.

Early next summer, the beavers had four more kits. Throughout the summer and fall, the five older ones helped their father make the lodge bigger and hollow out a third entrance tunnel. They added to the dam to make the pond wider and deeper, and collected a large food store.

That winter, the lodge was very crowded even though it was bigger. In summer the mother beaver was expecting another litter. There would be no room then for the eldest kits. They would only be in their mother's way. So she drove them away with nips and nudges.

In time they would find mates for themselves and start their own lodges. Their kits would do the same in their turn: dam streams, build lodges and bring up families of their own.

Beaver Facts

Teeth
Large, orange-coated teeth can fell a small tree in minutes

Ears and Nose
Can both be shut by special valves when the beaver dives

Coat
Waterproof and thick to keep out the cold

Tail
Broad and scaly. Used as a rudder when swimming, as a support when cutting trees, and to give a warning when danger threatens

Front Feet
Strong fingers and claws, are used for digging and for handling logs when building

Hind Feet
Webbed for swimming. Two of the claws are split down the middle and are used for combing the fur

Heavyweight Gnawers

The beaver belongs to the very large group of mammals called rodents. This group also includes squirrels, porcupines, rats, mice, and guinea pigs. After the South American capybara, the beaver is the heaviest of all the rodents. A fully grown beaver can be more than a yard long, including its broad tail. It can weigh up to 80 pounds.

Like all rodents, the beaver has sharp, chisel-like front teeth. Using these teeth and their powerful jaw muscles, a pair of beavers take less than 15 minutes to gnaw right through a tree trunk 4 inches thick.

Down by the Riverside

Beavers make their homes by rivers and lakes in forests where there are deciduous trees, such as aspens and alders. They feed on the inner bark of these trees, as well as on many small waterside plants. They are especially fond of water-lilies.

The Family Engineering Business

Beavers always live in family groups, with a mother and father and up to about a dozen young. Every member of the family helps with the building and repair of the dam and lodge. The animals are born engineers. They know instinctively how to cut down a tree and drive stakes into the river bed to start a dam. During the two years that the young stay with their parents, however, they learn even more about the craft of building. This means that they can make perfect dams when they go off to start their own colonies.

A beaver dam often stretches for two or three hundred yards and contains hundreds of tons of wood.

Slaughtered for Fur

Beavers were once common. But now they are found in only a few places because so many were killed for their fur and for the oily liquid which they use to mark their territories. This was used as a medicine. Beaver-hunting is now carefully controlled and their numbers are increasing.

A view of the beaver's dam and lodge from the air. You can see the canal they had to cut to get more wood.